T0193676

24 QUALITIES
—— THAT ——
HELPED ME
IMPROVE
MY LIFE

DAN SWEETMAN

BALBOA.PRESS

A DIVISION OF HAY HOUSE

Balboa Press books may be ordered through booksellers or by contacting:

Balboa Press
A Division of Hay House
1663 Liberty Drive
Bloomington, IN 47403
www.balboapress.com
1 (877) 407-4847

Because of the dynamic nature of the Internet, any web addresses or links contained in this book may have changed since publication and may no longer be valid. The views expressed in this work are solely those of the author and do not necessarily reflect the views of the publisher, and the publisher hereby disclaims any responsibility for them.

The author of this book does not dispense medical advice or prescribe the use of any technique as a form of treatment for physical, emotional, or medical problems without the advice of a physician, either directly or indirectly. The intent of the author is only to offer information of a general nature to help you in your quest for emotional and spiritual well-being. In the event you use any of the information in this book for yourself, which is your constitutional right, the author and the publisher assume no responsibility for your actions.

Any people depicted in stock imagery provided by Getty Images are models, and such images are being used for illustrative purposes only. Certain stock imagery © Getty Images.

Print information available on the last page.

ISBN: 978-1-9822-4514-6 (sc)
ISBN: 978-1-9822-4513-9 (e)

Balboa Press rev. date: 03/16/2020

Contents

Dedication

This book is dedicated to my mother and my father for the many gifts that they gave to me as I grew into a man. To my dad, I would like to say thank you for teaching me how to love and respect God, and to learn the Holy Scriptures. Thank you for teaching me to be honest, and to be a stand-up guy. Thank you for helping me to overcome my fear of public speaking.

To my mother, I am so very thankful and grateful to you for offering me the gift of music and song. Thank you for the many years of piano lessons, voice lessons, and the opportunity to learn orchestra theory and songwriting. Thank you for believing in me when I started writing and recording songs. Thank you for supporting me through all of the heartaches that came my way and for never giving up on me.

My parents were my greatest teachers and both of them still hold a very dear place in my heart. In the end, I buried my father when I was only thirty-three years old, and fifteen years later after suffering a long illness, I buried my mother. My mother once said to me that the way you keep someone alive long after they are gone is to talk about them. I suppose this is my way of keeping them alive through me. Although their physical bodies may be gone, their spirits and their love live on in me and my sisters, who have become the beneficiaries of their love and their wisdom.

Peace.

Introduction

Namaste!

The gesture Namaste represents the belief that there is a Divine spark within each human being that is located in the heart chakra. This gesture is an acknowledgment of the soul in one by the soul in another. The word *Nama* means bow, *as* means I, and *te* means you. Therefore, *namaste* literally means "bow me you" or "I bow to you." [1] For me this is a reminder that we all originated from greatness and when our earthly containers expire, we will all return to the same greatness that we came from. It is with this belief that I share this little book with you. Because we are what we came from, we all have the opportunity to tap into the divine essence of our beginning and find that greatness within us and be all that we are.

The following little essays are part of an ongoing observation that I have been watching over the years on how my life has been lived up until this point, and the

---

[1] https://www.yogajournal.com/practice/the-meaning-of-quot-namaste-quot

things that I have learned over the past five and a half decades through the relationships that I have had with my family, friends, coworkers, people in my community and society as a whole. One of the most rewarding things that can happen to us as progressive human beings is to actually become better with age and experience, and find the grace to know it, or at least believe it. I'm not speaking of any ego here, rather an honest understanding and acceptance of the progress made as an individual on this planet. The flip side to this, however, is recognizing where we may have fallen short for the many years that we have lived, and how we have treated not only our own life, but also the lives of others that were part of our circle. Take heart, if you've fallen short, you're human. If you've made mistakes, you're human. If you've lost friendships, you're human. But don't despair, change is a part of life and every day that we awake gives us another opportunity to change. In fact, the only constant there is--is change!

This guidebook is not meant to be a reminder of where we've fallen short, or the mistakes that we've made, but rather a reminder of the things that most of us have been taught and most of us know instinctively by nature, nurture and community. The following lessons were taught to us over the span of our lives, but it never hurts to learn a little bit more about ourselves with each passing day. Think of these short lessons as a "refresher course" in the basics of human interaction that we learned as children and as young adults. Perhaps they will bring to mind a few time-honored truths that can only edify us when put into our daily routine. At the end of each essay you have an opportunity to put into practice each of these lessons, whether it be in meditation or in action. Either way, by reintegrating these truths into our lives on a daily basis can only affect us for the good. Many philosophies teach that we originated from a single source of perfection, full of wisdom, integrity and light. Remember, we are what we came from. All we need to do is to act that way every day and bring the light of love and perfection back to the world, one person at a time, one deed at a time, and one day at a time.

Although this book can be read in one sitting, the lessons here are not meant to be rushed through, but rather read one day at a time and meditate on each one and putting that one daily lesson into practice, if possible. One of the most difficult things to do as humans is to admit that we have faults and flaws in our life. It must stem from our basic need for self-preservation and looking out for number one first. However, the only way to properly fix and rectify something that's not functioning correctly is to clearly identify the cause, and then devise a solution or a work-around for the problem. I have learned that as we age, we become more tolerant to things that used to set us off or irritate us when we were younger. It's all part of the "mellowing" process. I've also noticed in my own life that when I was younger, I put a greater emphasis on working on the *outside* of who I was. I had to look my best, nice hair, nice clothes, nice car and so on. But as I have aged and grown a little wiser, I have made a gradual shift to place more energy on the *inside* traits and characteristics, like the qualities that follow in these short essays. These lessons have become part of my journey to help me be the best version of myself that I can while I have the gift of breath and life. May these words also inspire you and uplift you to be the best version of yourself. Namaste!

1

BE THANKFUL

When you rise in the morning, give thanks for the light, for your life, for your strength. Give thanks for your food and for the joy of living. If you see no reason to give thanks, the fault lies in yourself. – Tecumseh

From the moment that we wake up there is so much to be thankful for and we need to be reminded of this. For starters--you woke up! This is not to be taken lightly whatsoever. Open the Obituary section of any morning paper and you will realize very quickly that today you have a gift that not one of those people listed will have ever again. You are here--six feet this side of the grass. That should be all it takes to get you in a place to be thankful for life and breath, right now--at this very moment. If you have decent to moderate health, be thankful. If your health is less than great, be thankful that you have time to change and get better. If all of your five senses are working correctly today, be thankful. If you have a spouse, friends, or someone to love, be thankful. If you have a family, parents, children, brothers, sisters, aunts, uncles, pets, be thankful. If you have a nice place to live, whether it be a house, a condo, an apartment, or even a hovel, be thankful. If it's cold today and you have heat, be thankful. If it's over 100 degrees and you have central air, be thankful. If you have hot water to take a warm shower, be thankful. If you have food in the cabinets and the refrigerator, be thankful. If you are getting ready for work and have a job, be thankful. If you have a vehicle to get you to work that is still in running condition, be thankful. By asking these questions it can make us aware of what we actually do have that should remind us to always be thankful. It is quite possible that if you were to list everything that you have to be thankful for, that list would be much longer than you think. And for that--be thankful!

The point of this exercise is to realize that we have much to be thankful and instead of letting days, weeks, months or even years go by without ever acknowledging what you have been blessed with, start to remind yourself every single day just how much you actually do have, and be thankful for everything always, right now at this moment. Try to say the words "thank you" at least once a day to something or someone greater than you, whether it be God, Buddha, a higher power, or just to the universe.

I realize that life can be difficult at times and it's hard to be in a grateful mood when you've hit the valley floor, but this is where our inner strength lies. To be able to be positive and thankful in the throes of anxiety or deep depression, is where our true character lies. In my own experience, when I find myself in one of these dark places, I still try and find the strength inside of me to say thank you each morning that I awake. I still try and wear a smile when I am out in public, and I still try to remain positive even if I can't find a shred of hope anywhere. I remind myself, this too shall pass, and keep moving in the forward direction. As long as there is breath, there is hope, and as long as I have another day to wake up and live my life, I am thankful for one more opportunity.

I remember hearing a quote years ago by Helen Keller that quite possibly many of us heard from our parents or perhaps a teacher that went something like this: "I once felt bad because I had no shoes, until I met a man that had no feet." I'm sure this piece of wisdom was shared with us to impress upon us the importance of always being grateful and thankful for everything that we have, because there is always going to be someone else out there less fortunate than ourselves, and quite possibly in worse condition than we are. Remember, today is a gift, and definitely something to be thankful for.

When I was a young twenty-something I was driving through town and my car broke down in front of a local cemetery. I walked to a gas station down the road and called my dad's pager--yes, I said pager. Remember, this was the early 1980's. I left the phone number of the payphone and waited for his call back. When the phone rang, I picked it up and I asked him for help, I told him where I was, and he said he would be down in a few minutes. When he arrived, he saw how frustrated I was, but he was just smiling at me. I asked him what was so funny, and he shared with me another teachable moment.

He went on to say that throughout his life, when he was feeling lost or abandoned, or unsure what direction he was to go, he would visit a cemetery and walk through the rows and read some of the headstones. Being surrounded by death put his own life in a new perspective, and he would say a silent prayer of thanksgiving for his life and the opportunities that he still had. This was his reminder that we are never to treat this precious gift lightly, and that the alternative was staring him right in the face. His advice to me was simple- perhaps God allowed my car to break down here, in front of a cemetery, to teach me to always be thankful for life and for breath. The car can be fixed, so not to worry. That moment made such an impression on me, that to this day, each time I drive by a cemetery, I say a silent prayer of thanks that I still have a gift that no one that has passed will ever have again.

Today may be a good opportunity to pick one or two people in your life that you are grateful for, and that you appreciate having in your life and letting them know it. That one gesture may be just the thing that someone needs to hear today to feel wanted, needed and appreciated.

If you are really thankful, what do you do? You share. – W. Clement Stone

2

BE KIND

Kindness is the language which the deaf can hear and the blind can see. —Mark Twain

Ancient Chinese philosopher and writer Lao Tzu once said, *"Kindness in words creates confidence. Kindness in thinking creates profoundness. Kindness in giving creates love."* When a person is kind, any preconceived walls of doubt and fear seem to crumble and fade away. Kindness is a powerful force with long lasting ripple effects. Lebanese poet and writer Kahlil Gibran also noted that *"Kindness is like snow- It beautifies everything it covers."* Some people may see kindness as a form of weakness, not being tough enough. If you're too kind you will get taken advantage of and misused. But this could also become an excuse that we tell ourselves just so we don't have to be so kind toward others.

Everyone today seems so busy and so preoccupied; it feels like people barely notice each other anymore. Most people that I encounter on a daily basis have their eyes and their attention glued to their mobile devices, and many are not even aware of their surroundings. When you're that preoccupied, you don't have time in your schedule to interact with anyone else. In days of old when people would be out and about they would greet others that they saw and strike up a short conversation. It was a time when people went out to engage with others, not bury their faces in a screen. The opportunities for human kindness seemed to abound back then, but it doesn't seem to be that way anymore. Society as a whole seems to be a little more antisocial than it was when I was growing up.

I consider myself to be a kind person. After all, I've had many years of practice. Being in sales can be a two-edged sword at times when dealing with customers. Some, are like the heavens opened and dropped the nicest, most understanding angel of a person right in your lap, while other times it seems that nasty gremlins escaped from the seventh circle of hell with only one mission, and that's to make your life absolutely miserable, for as long as humanly possible. In both scenarios, I have always tried to keep my cool and maintain my own inner peace, but as a mere mortal, sadly, I have failed and let them get the best of me every now and again. I have always been kind to the kind, and as much as humanly possible, kind to the unkind. Some have thought of me as weak because I chose not to engage the unkind people, however, I have always believed that holding one's peace is a sign of true inner strength.

President Franklin Roosevelt said that *"Human kindness has never weakened the stamina or softened the fiber of a free people. A nation does not have to be cruel to be tough."* People who are kind can be just as tough to hold their own, tough enough to not get taken for, and tough enough to get the job done. Practice kindness every day. It not only blesses the person receiving it, but it blesses the giver as well. Be a giver of kindness and watch for miracles.

According to <u>Kindness Health Facts:</u> *Kindness is contagious. The positive effects of kindness are experienced in the brain of everyone who witnessed the act, improving their mood and making them significantly more likely to "pay it forward." This means one good deed in a crowded area can create a domino effect and improve the day of dozens of people! Kindness increases the love hormone, energy, happiness, life span, pleasure and serotonin. Kindness also decreases pain, stress, anxiety, depression and blood pressure.*[2]

Being kind improves one's health and overall well-being. Being kind can inspire others to do the same. Today, be an example and practice kindness by greeting a stranger with a smile or wishing someone you meet good health. Take an interest in someone that you meet today, and spend a few minutes talking with them and listening to them. We never know who we are going to meet on any given day, and just one simple act of kindness on our part can affect someone for good and change their outlook on life.

---

[2] https://www.dartmouth.edu/wellness/emotional/rakhealthfacts.pdf

A show of kindness can heal wounds that no words could ever reach. Practice being kind. All you'll feel is good!

You cannot do a kindness too soon, for you never know how soon it will be too late. -Ralph Waldo Emerson

3

BE APPRECIATIVE

As we express our gratitude, we must never forget that the highest appreciation is not to utter words, but to live by them.
— John F. Kennedy

When is the last time that you said the words, "I appreciate you" to someone special in your life? How many people affect your life on a given day, that without them, your life would not be as rich and fulfilling as it is? When someone is there for us to help us, to comfort us, or just be there for us, we should remember to let them know that we appreciate them. It's been said that we don't know what we have until it's gone, but if we live by that standard, then it's already too late. Why not start showing appreciation and letting the people in our lives know just how much they mean to us.

Many years ago, my dad asked me if I had ever tipped my garbage man. I was a bit surprised by the question, but I responded, no. He then asked me to try it on an upcoming holiday and hand the driver an envelope with $20 in it and thank him for his service and tell him that you appreciate the job that he is doing. After all, my dad went on to say, we need people who will collect our garbage and dispose of it for us. We should appreciate these people. When the next holiday approached, I heard the truck coming down the street and I ran out to meet him. When he stopped to see what I wanted, I handed him an envelope and told him this was a little gift to say thank you for the job that he is doing. He was so grateful that he just sat there speechless for a moment and then went on to say that I was the first person on his route to ever give him a holiday bonus. My dad certainly knew how to bring the best out of someone. For many years after that, I continued to tip our garbage man, and even if we forgot to put the barrels out, he would get out of his truck, walk down our driveway and empty our cans for us. I guess he never forgot that little gesture that we did to let him know how just much we appreciate the job that he does for us.

There's a short anonymous poem that I read years ago that starts out like this:

"If you're ever going to love me love me now, while I can know, all the sweet and tender feelings from which real affection flow. Love me now, while I am living; do not wait until I am gone, and then chisel it in marble — warm love words on ice-cold stone."

Take a moment right now and think of five people who are in your life every day and how they touch your life with kindness, compassion and love for you. Spend a few moments in meditation today and send positive thoughts to them and then when you see them in person, tell them that you appreciate them. Every person needs encouragement, even if you think they don't. People also need validation-- for their feelings their actions and their struggles. It only takes a moment to let them know, but the effect that it will have on them will last long after your kind words are spoken.

Today, have an inner appreciation for your loved ones, your friends and your family, but also have an appreciation for life and the beauty of it. Maybe you would like to try tipping your garbage person on the next holiday and be sure to thank them for the job they're doing. You'll be surprised how such a small gesture on your part can change a person's day, week or even their life.

Remember, yesterday is gone, today is here, and tomorrow is not guaranteed. Make the most of what you have by showing appreciation for everything you are, everything you have and everyone close to you.

"If you haven't all the things you want, be grateful for the things you don't have that you wouldn't want." — Unknown

4

BE GENEROUS

We must give more in order to get more. It is the generous giving of ourselves that produces the generous harvest. — Orison Swett Marden

When I was a young twenty-something, my mother tried teaching me this lesson on generosity. She said, "God cannot fill your basket if it is already full, so empty your basket." My mother's wise words painted a picture for me that has stayed with me to this day. Throughout my life I have lived by this principle of giving whenever I can, many times to my dismay and my heartache. I have learned over the years that not everyone that I met or helped had genuine motives or an honest need, but rather they saw me as an opportunity for them to take advantage of a "giver", or in my case--a "sucker.".

Dr. Christiane Northrup in 'Dodging Energy Vampires' notes that *"Highly sensitive people—or empaths—see life through the eyes of compassion and caring. They were born that way. As a result, they carry a tremendous amount of inner light. But they're also the favored prey of "vampires" who feed off empaths' energy and disrupt their lives on every level— physical, emotional, and financial."*

I have learned that there is a very fine line between being a "giver" and being a "sucker", and that can be the reason that many generous people stop giving over the years because they do not want to be taken advantage of. It's too bad when this happens because there may have been genuine needs that required our attention, but due to past experiences we instead shied away because of self-preservation. Regardless of any past negative experiences with being generous, I still choose to be unselfish and to help when I can. My eyes are more open now than they were years ago, but I still have an innocence when it comes to helping people, still holding to the belief that most people are inherently good, and want the same decent quality of life that we all strive for.

As a Christian, I believe in the concept of tithing, or *paying it forward.* The Bible teaches that we are to give a percentage of our wealth or bounty as a way of thanksgiving for all of the blessings bestowed upon us. It's a reminder that we are blessed in order to be able to help others. Although tithing to a church may be one way to accomplish this, the reality is that we can tithe in many ways including volunteering of our time to organizations that help individuals down on their luck perhaps. It's up to the individual on how to pay their generosity forward.

Chances are, we have many opportunities to practice generosity, whether it be giving a little something to the homeless person on the side of the road asking for help, or responding to our local community services asking for donations to help feed hungry families in need right in our own hometown. It has been said that we are our brother's keeper and it's up to all of us to look out for each of us. Native Americans believe that by giving generously brings people closer together and can strengthen one's commitment to the community. Native Americans also feel honored when someone asks something of them. Although the act of asking is an act of vulnerability, it gives them the chance to become closer to each other and to show their commitment to the relationship.

Today, find opportunities to be generous and to give something of value, whether it be material or not. Not every act of giving has to involve the exchange of material possessions. In fact, most of the time when you give of yourself, your time and your kindness, it is those gifts that have the most lasting effect on someone long after the material objects have tarnished and faded.

The heart that gives, gathers. — Lao Tzu, Tao Te Ching

5

BE FORGIVING

The weak can never forgive. Forgiveness is an attribute of the strong. — Mahatma Gandhi

In most major religions, forgiveness is also one of the four qualities attributed to the Creator or The Supreme Being along with love, mercy and compassion. These four qualities comprise the full essence of a god-like person. In The Lord's Prayer, Jesus taught that we should forgive those who have trespassed against us, just as we are forgiven for the trespasses we have done against God.[3] Because we all need forgiveness at some point in our lives, the lesson here is to learn how to also forgive. How can we ever expect to be forgiven, if we are unwilling to forgive others? As long as we live in human flesh, we are bound to make mistakes and unintentionally hurt the ones we love. We may even hurt strangers by our actions, by our speech and by our negligence, but as long as there is room for forgiveness, there are opportunities for growth. I heard

---

[3] Mt. 6:9-13 King James Version

it once said that as long as there is breath, there is hope. Oh, how true this is.

One of the hardest things for us to do as human beings is to find forgiveness for those who have wronged us terribly, but even more so, to find a way to forgive ourselves for our own wrongdoings. When I was young, my father said that the best way for a person to learn forgiveness is to need it. The same goes for mercy and compassion. If we have been the recipient of forgiveness at some point in our life, chances are that it helped us to become more forgiving and move forward, learning from our past. Forgiving others is as much for you as it is for the one being forgiven. While they may feel a sense of absolution, you will feel a sense of peace. When we forgive and let go of anger, hatred, and the seeking of revenge against the one who harmed us, we become stronger and more empowered. Nelson Mandela is quoted saying, "Forgiveness liberates the soul. It removes fear. That is why it is such a powerful weapon."

We've all heard the term 'forgive and forget', but how many of us can actually live by this guiding principle? The Bible teaches that when God forgives someone of their sins, '[he] casts their sins into the depths of the sea'[4], and it goes on to say that 'their sins and iniquities will I remember no more.'[5] True forgiveness has built into it the ability to forget and move forward. This is also an attribute of Almighty God. This is an attribute of the strong. Remember, the weak can never forgive.

---

[4] Mi. 7:19 King James Version
[5] He. 10:17 King James Version

Today, spend some time in quiet meditation and search your mind, your heart, and your soul for anyone in your past and your present that may need your forgiveness. Do you need to forgive yourself for something that you did to another? If you find that there are areas of your life that need your attention, send thoughts of forgiveness to those who may have hurt you and remember to also send thoughts of forgiveness to yourself.

He that cannot forgive others breaks the bridge over which he himself must pass if he would ever reach heaven; for everyone has need to be forgiven. —George Herbert

6

BE ADVENTUROUS

Security is mostly a superstition. It does not exist in nature, nor do the children of men as a whole experience it. Avoiding danger is no safer in the long run than outright exposure. Life is either a daring adventure, or nothing. — Helen Keller

Merriam-Webster defines adventure as *'an undertaking usually involving danger and unknown risks'*, and adventurous as *'disposed to seek adventure or to cope with the new and unknown'*. It is in this spirit that I sit and write this short essay. Most of us, as we journey through life find solace in our own "comfort zone" and we settle into a routine that's predictable and manageable, for the most part. There's nothing wrong with this as we all seek and want structure and stability, but I wonder if sometimes we allow that structure to hinder our own personal sense of adventure.

Some of the most exciting times in my life was when I took chances and threw caution to the wind, trying something new, something with some element of inherent danger--not so much to get hurt, but to seek an unknown thrill that I had never tried before. When I was a boy, I tried skiing for the first time and it was absolutely exhilarating, and I wanted more of it. My first-time water-skiing was also a total blast and my dad had to drag me out of the lake because I didn't want it to end. When I was a teen, I rode a motorcycle for the first time, and that too was some kind of awesome for me and still is to this day. There is this kind of life education we get where we experience things outside of our comfort zone, not in any classroom, but out in the real world.

As we get older, perhaps the chances we take are more in line with personal, business or financial risks, but still there is a sense of adventure in these types of experiences as well. Taking chances on financial investments without having any guarantee that you won't lose everything that you have invested can be just as risky as water-skiing behind a fast power boat or setting up an online dating profile if you're over fifty. Again, it's the fear of the unknown that keeps us from trying new things and stepping out a little and taking that risk. But it is also in these moments that we can overcome some of that fear making us more likely to try something new again. It's all about baby steps.

Today, find a way to be adventurous. It doesn't have to be anything dangerous that could hurt you, but it should be something outside your comfort zone. Maybe try making one new friend this week, or perhaps you could take a train to work instead of driving your car. Maybe the next time someone asks you to go somewhere new with them you say "yes" instead of "no". How about taking a long drive this weekend with your spouse, friend or significant other and make no plans on where to go. Just find a road and let it take you to wherever-- stop for lunch, enjoy the scenery, stop and take photos, treat yourselves to an ice cream, enjoy dinner and find the back roads home. No maps, no GPS, no plans. Of course, if you get lost, you'll most likely still have your cell phone and still be able to find your way home. Sounds like fun doesn't it? Make it an adventure that you won't soon forget!

Twenty years from now you will be more disappointed by the things you didn't do than by the ones you did. So throw off the bowlines. Sail away from the safe harbor. Catch the trade winds in your sails. Explore. Dream. Discover. —Mark Twain

7

BE COMPASSIONATE

One of the secrets of inner peace is the practice of compassion.
—Dalai Lama

Compassion is defined as a feeling of deep sympathy for another who is stricken by misfortune, accompanied by a strong desire to alleviate the suffering. Best-selling author and motivational speaker Steve Maraboli is quoted saying "A kind gesture can reach a wound that only compassion can heal."

There is extensive research that shows that people who are compassionate to other human beings as well as animals, have a longer lifespan than their non-compassionate counterpart. Genuine compassion that stems from an altruistic behavior rather than a self-serving behavior can also improve the recovery time when a person is ill, improve their optimism, improve their social interaction, and boost their overall psychological well-being.[6] Another benefit to being a compassionate person is the tendency to redirect the focus away from ourselves and our own problems and shift to a concern for others who may be experiencing heartache, loss, or sadness.

Compassionate people also show a deep respect and appreciation for all living creatures, which, because recent studies show that animals can actually feel many of the same emotions that humans feel. In his book *"Beyond Words: What Animals Think and Feel"*, Carl Safina shares some of his research on this topic and surprisingly we as humans are not that different from animals. They have a wide range of emotions as we do, and they can feel when someone is kind and when someone is cruel. Even King Solomon said, "The godly care for their animals, but the wicked are always cruel." [7] Mahatma Gandhi said, *"The greatness of a nation can be measured by the way its animals are treated."*

Compassionate people also care for the environment, from plants and trees, to the air that we breathe, to the fresh water that we drink. All humans are born from nature needing the same resources that all plants need. We need the sun to provide energy and warmth, we need fresh air and water to exist, and we need minerals from the soil to live long, healthy lives. It is our duty to protect all of our natural resources from greedy profiteers who would just

---

[6] https://www.onegreenplanet.org/animalsandnature/how-showing-compassion-for-animals-can-improve-your-health/

[7] Pr. 12:10 New Living Translation

as soon destroy the planet without any concern for future generations relying on our precious resources.

People are not born compassionate. Compassion is a human trait that is learned through upbringing, through involvement in the community and by practice. The more compassionate we become; the more opportunities seem to present themselves to us. Today find a way to be compassionate. Whether an animal needs some loving, a human being needs some encouragement, or a flower needs a thank you and a stroke of its petals, practice compassion today.

If you have men who will exclude any of God's creatures from the shelter of compassion and pity, you will have men who will deal likewise with their fellow men. —Francis of Assisi

8

BE ON TIME

Preparedness and punctuality are two of the most important qualities of a leader. — John A. Widtsoe

One personality trait that I find most annoying is when someone is not punctual. When I was young my parents taught me that being on time is extremely important. They encouraged me to be a few minutes early as a way to always be on time. I have practiced this trait for all of my adult life and in my humble opinion it has served me well. I see being on time as respect for others and a respect for their time. If I make someone wait for me, it feels like I am sending a message that my own time is more important than theirs. For both business and personal appointments, this may cause the meeting to start off on a bad footing, and if it can be avoided, then I suppose being on time is the answer.

The best way that I have found to be on time is to start with your appointment time and then work your day backwards as a means of knowing when to do what, so as to stay on schedule and not be late. This is the best way that I have found to stick to a schedule and always be on time. It also fosters better organizational skills because it helps you write down your daily events and determine how much time is needed to accomplish the tasks that you have on your calendar for the day. I have worked in sales for years and one thing that I have seen is by being on time, customers appreciate the respect and it helps to create a conducive environment for openness and an opportunity to close the job. I understand that in real life situations arise and we end up running late. I get it-- things happen. But we all carry cell phones with us, and it only takes a minute or so to call and let the other party know that you are running late, and you will be there as soon as you can. At least the waiting party is now aware of your situation and when to expect you. This shows tremendous respect and a concern for others' time. By not calling and letting them know that you are running late is just rude and will undoubtedly have an adverse effect on the appointment.

If you are struggling with being on time, pick a day this week and try to be early for every appointment, every get-together and most importantly, your job. Plan ahead, make a schedule, and stick to it. Think of the reasons that cause you to be late so often and find a way to overcome them. If you have a hard time getting out of bed, try getting up half an hour earlier and force yourself to do it. If you carpool or rideshare to work and the rideshare people are always late, find another way to get to work. If you just don't think that it's that important, reconsider how disrespectful and self-serving that way of thinking is and change. People tend to gravitate towards reliable, dependable people. If you want to succeed in life and in your business endeavors, be on time.

Successful people are invariably dependable. People can rely on them. Successful people keep their commitments. — Brian Tracy, Self-help author and speaker

9

BE A FRIEND

If you go looking for a friend, you're going to find they're very scarce. If you go out to be a friend, you'll find them everywhere. – Zig Ziglar

When we are youngsters it seems that just about everyone we hang around with or play with are our friends, and for the most part that's probably true. They are part of our young community because of school, sports, or summer vacations. But as we grow into our teens, we begin to learn a little more on what friendship is and we become more selective about the people we hang around with. As we mature into adulthood with our growing years behind us, our past experiences have most likely educated us on the type of friends that we really want, as well as the type of people that we do not want in our lives.

I've heard it said that if we can count the number of true friends on one hand, then we are considered most blessed. So, what's involved in finding the right kind of long-lasting friendships? King Solomon noted in his Proverbs that "a man that has friends must himself be friendly". [8] Like the quote above from Zig Ziglar, if you go out to be a friend to people you meet, you will inevitably find new friends. One of the key ingredients in any friendship is communication or staying in touch. With today's modern cell phone and computer technology it's easier than it has ever been. Right now, in a matter of seconds we can talk to anyone anywhere in the world with our cell phones. We can text long messages, we can send photos and videos, we can share our favorite song, and we can be there 'in spirit' keeping our friendships alive. When I was a kid growing up in the early 1970's, houses had one landline telephone, answering machines had not yet been invented, and if you wanted to reach a friend in another state, you would have to sit down and hand write a card or letter, address the envelope, buy a stamp and mail it. If you were lucky that letter made it there in about a week. Of course, you had no idea if your friend ever received the letter unless they called your home phone or wrote you back. It seems so antiquated now but it still has a certain charm for me.

Back then, the most common way to spend time with a friend was to get on my bike and ride to his or her house and ring the doorbell. We had no cell phones, so texting was not an option, video games would not be invented for another twelve or so years, so we played outside for hours until dark. Of those early friendships, one or two kids stayed close to me until our family moved. The loss of those friends saddened me at that time, but as children,

---

[8] Pr. 18:24 New King James Version

we were so resilient, that as soon as we got settled into our new home, my sisters and I made friends very quickly, as most children do. Many of those friendships lasted for years until life events changed the dynamics and we found out who were our true friends and who were not.

If you are blessed to have a few great friends, let them know that you appreciate them. Thank them for being such an important part of your life. If you are struggling with finding the right people to bring into your life, try being a friend to someone without expecting anything in return. Think of the qualities that you would like in your friends, and then try as much as possible to emulate those same qualities.

Lots of people want to ride with you in the limo, but what you want is someone who will take the bus with you when the limo breaks down. — Oprah Winfrey

10

BE UNDERSTANDING

Any fool can criticize, condemn, and complain but it takes character and self-control to be understanding and forgiving.
—Dale Carnegie

What does it mean to be understanding? Merriam-Webster defines it as 'a mental grasp, or the power to comprehend'. Although there are many versions to the saying *Walk a mile in his shoes*, the common message being conveyed is, that before you set out to judge someone, or find fault with someone, you must first understand his or her experiences, their challenges and their thought processes[9], hence, walking a mile in their shoes. There is no possible way to understand what another person has gone through or is going through, unless we ourselves have also gone through, or are going through similar experiences. Most of us can tell when someone truly understands what we are going through and those who are just mouthing the words 'I understand'.

---

[9] https://grammarist.com/phrase/walk-a-mile-in-someone-elses-shoes/

Real understanding goes beyond mental comprehension though. It has built into it real-life, genuine experiences felt on a cellular level with all of the emotions present, both good and bad, at the time of such experiences. Think of it as a *'been there, done that'* moment. To be understanding means developing an ability to listen more and speak less. In my experience, when someone is trying to share difficult or emotional events with me, they're really just looking for someone that will listen to them without judging them and without offering unsolicited advice. Honesty is always the best option at moments like these. If I have not experienced what they are going through, when asked to say something, I let them know that I don't know what they are going through, but as a friend, I am here to listen and offer comfort as much as possible. To say "I understand what you're dealing with" means that you have experienced something very similar or identical to what they have just shared with you. If that's not the case, then don't say it. Most of us can tell when we people are being less than honest with us, and it could have a negative impact on the relationship.

B.J. Neblett is quoted saying *"We are the sum total of our experiences. Those experiences – be they positive or negative – make us the person we are, at any given point in our lives."* It is these experiences that help us when dealing with others that may be going through some or all of what we went through. Because we walked it, felt it, and experienced it, we are in a much better position to say the words "I understand" and let others feel the power behind our words, not just empty platitudes.

If you want to understand people better, try putting into practice these helpful tips. First, think before you speak. It's good to take a deep breath or two and think about what you want to say. Second, listen more and speak less, otherwise the conversation becomes all about you instead of the other person. Third, when you speak, get to the point quickly without belaboring, and don't talk just to hear yourself speak. Last, mean what you say, and say what you mean. Being understanding doesn't always mean that you have to agree with someone. You can understand and still disagree. People respect honesty. By becoming more understanding can also help us to be better understood.

If we are to live together in peace, we must come to know each other better."— Lyndon Johnson

11

BE BOLD

Be bold. Do what the ordinary fear. — Anonymous

It has been said that *fortune favors the bold* [10], meaning those who face problems or tasks with courage and determination without backing down, are usually the ones who achieve massive success. We can see this in our own lives as well. The times in our life that we backed down showed our weakness and our fear, and the times that we spoke up and took chances, going against the grain, showed our strength and our willingness to never give up.

Human beings are not born bold. We learn boldness through action and practice. There are a few things you can do to become bold where others may run for cover. First off, be real. Say what's on your mind regardless of what others may think. Be willing to take the road less traveled while everyone else walks the well-worn path.

---

[10] Quote attributed to James Swartz

Those who are bold throw caution to the wind more often than not, willing to do what others are too scared to do.

Second, learn from your mistakes. Being bold means learning from your failures. If things don't work out the first time, do not quit! Get up and try, try again. If you're stuck, ask someone who is better at this task for their help. At some point you will succeed by not giving up. I've had many experiences throughout my life where I have had the opportunity to be bold, and stand up for what I believe in. Being bold doesn't mean being pushy, it just means that you don't back down when the going gets tough. Instead, you fight harder to win.

If you're wondering if you're bold enough, ask yourself, *"Am I willing to try new things that I've never done before?"* This is a great way to practice being bold. You're allowed to be afraid of trying new things, but are you able to overcome your fears? Years ago, a friend of mine always wanted to learn rock climbing. He and I would walk the trails up the mountain near the reservoir close to where we had lived. He would stop and watch the climbers as they scaled the cliffs and I saw how excited this made him, but he also shared with me his fears of falling. I could tell he was a little scared, but I encouraged him to go for it and look for classes and join one already. A few weeks later he told me that he had signed up for a beginner's rock-climbing course. What a great way to overcome fear and practice being bold all at the same time.

Today, be honest. Be yourself. Try something new. Encourage a complete stranger. There are opportunities all around us for us to practice being bold. There is a sense of peace and freedom that fills us when we are willing to be bold. Today, be extraordinary. Today, be bold!

Whatever you can do, or dream you can, begin it. Boldness has genius, power and magic in it. —Johann Wolfgang von Goethe

12

BE HUMBLE

Be strong, but not rude. Be kind, but not weak. Be bold, but don't bully. Be humble, but not shy. Be confident, but not arrogant. [11]

The word *humble* originates from the Latin word, *humilis*, meaning low. Merriam-Webster defines humble as *not proud or haughty; not arrogant or assertive.* Also, *insignificant and unpretentious.* So, can a person be both bold and humble at the same time? The simple answer is yes. A person who is bold possesses an inner strength and knowledge. By not seeking praise or honor from others for such qualities, one remains humble. So how do we go about learning to be humble?

If we look back throughout history there are many examples of people who were bold in the face of all types of adverse situations yet remained humble and at peace

[11] https://www.lifehack.org/articles/lifestyle/strong-kind-bold-humble-and-confident.html

within themselves. Examples that come to mind are Jesus Christ, Paul an apostle of Jesus, Mother Teresa, Mahatma Gandhi, Nelson Mandela, and Martin Luther King. Each of these men and women had to be bold and stand strong in the face of the opposition, yet remain peaceful, non-violent, and humble. By following these examples, we too can learn to be humble and lowly, not seeking honor or praise for our deeds.

When I was in my twenties, I was outgoing, I was fun, and I was most certainly the life of the party. As the years have passed, the struggles and the heartaches of life that I have gone through have caused me to be less outgoing and more of a person who remains in the background for the most part, and out of the limelight as much as possible. I think that heartache has a way of not only crushing someone, but also mellowing and humbling a person. I know that I can be bold and strong when I need to be, but I prefer to stay low and under the radar as much as possible without forcing myself on anyone.

When I was younger, my mom gave me one of her little nuggets of parental wisdom. She said, *"When you truly know who you are, you don't have to tell anyone."* Meaning, when you possess a confidence and inner knowledge of your own abilities and talents, there's no need to boast about them because they will inevitably shine through, much of the time without your even knowing. Of the many self-help books that I have read, they all agree that the most effective leaders are the ones who encourage others to figure things out for themselves and find their own way. As Lao Tzu once said, *"To lead the people, walk behind them."*

The hardest part about learning to be humble is setting aside our own egos. Ego always wants to take center stage and always wants to dominate. Those who practice humility remain low and in the background much of the time, unless situations demand otherwise. The following is an excerpt from verse 66 of the Tao Te Ching; Why is the sea king of a hundred streams? Because it lies below them. Humility gives it its power. Therefore, those desiring a position above others must speak humble. Those desiring to lead must follow.

The only wisdom we can hope to acquire is the wisdom of humility. — T.S. Eliot

13

BE ENCOURAGING

It is time for us all to stand and cheer for the doer, the achiever – the one who recognizes the challenges and does something about it. — Vince Lombardi

I would imagine that most people have had an experience or two where they've felt discouraged about something. Maybe you were passed over for a promotion at your place of work? Maybe you've applied to numerous job opportunities and no one has called back? Perhaps someone that you trusted has let you down and you are now questioning the friendship. Whatever the case may be, there are many ways we can be left feeling discouraged. But on the flip side, how many of us have ever been encouraged to continue? How many times has a friend or relative encouraged us to try something new for the first time? How many times has someone said to you, *you can do it, I believe in you*?

It's one thing to experience being both discouraged and encouraged as we live our lives, but we must ask ourselves this question, how often do *we* discourage or encourage others? Do we leave people feeling forlorn and worse for wear, or do we leave people feeling better about themselves and that they can accomplish anything? There is a well-known poem that starts *"Is anybody happier because you passed their way?"* When we meet people what do they see? When we speak to them what do they hear? When we leave them, how do they feel? We all make an impact, but do we know what sort of impact we leave people with long after we are gone?

Encouragement is defined as *the action of giving someone support, confidence, or hope*[12], but I see it more as being the type of person to others that we would like people to be toward us. Basically, the golden rule which says, *do unto others, that you would have them do unto you*. We are all sojourners on this planet moving along a path from birth to death and dealing with all of life's experiences along the way. Each of us need encouragement and a 'vote of confidence' every now and then to keep us moving forward. If we are constantly bombarded with negative people and opinions that tear us down and destroy our confidence, it becomes quite difficult to muster the strength needed to keep going because all we end up feeling is despair.

When I am out in public and if someone is helping me or waiting on me and they are doing a great job, I make it a habit to tell them, and then I thank them for being so

---

[12] https://www.lexico.com/en/definition/encouragement

good at what they do. There's no harm in giving someone a little encouragement for doing their job and letting them know that you noticed. I recently visited a big box retail store and I needed help finding an item down one of the aisles. After locating a store associate to help me, a young man led me directly to the item I was in search of and handed it to me. I shook his hand and told him how appreciative I was for his knowledge of the store and how polite he was to me. He beamed from ear to ear smiling and said he was just doing his job. I wish all store clerks did their job like that young man.

So how can we be more encouraging in our daily life? How can we leave people feeling better about themselves? There is much to read on this subject both in print and online[13], but basically everything points to a few basic principles that we can employ to be more encouraging to those that we encounter. First, show people that you are genuine and that you care about them. You can get to know more about someone by asking them questions about their life, their family, and their interests. This shows that you are interested in them and they will feel that you care about them. Second, show them. Maybe it's a greeting card sent for no reason whatsoever but has a few encouraging words on the inside. Perhaps it's a hug or a pat on the back showing your love and concern. When is the last time that you sent someone a bouquet of flowers for no reason at all other than to make them smile? Whatever the method, it's a sign to them confirming

---

[13] https://www.mattmcwilliams.com/how-to-encourage-others-and-inspire-your-followers/; https://thelife.com/19-ways-to-encourage-others

your words in action. Another way to encourage someone is to offer them real help. If someone is discouraged and going through a difficult time, you can ask them if they need your help and then offer to do whatever you can to alleviate their trouble.

Spend a day encouraging as many people as you can. Remember, encouragement is giving someone support, confidence or hope. You can do this. In doing so, you are putting positive energy back into the universe that will someday come back to you when you need it most.

People may forget what you said, but they will never forget how you made them feel.
—Carl W. Buehner

14

BE CONTENT

Be content with what you have; rejoice in the way things are.
When you realize there is nothing lacking, the whole world
belongs to you. —Lao Tzu

Although the quote above was written over twenty-five
hundred years ago, it still seems that humankind has
always been in a race for more. More wealth, more fame,
more stuff, more of anything and everything. When is
enough, enough? It seems that the more time we waste
pursuing the things that we don't have, the less time we
have to actually enjoy the things that we already possess.
So many people end up striving instead of arriving. Why
is this? Perhaps our society has placed too big an emphasis
on getting and achieving more, and less of an emphasis
on being grateful for what we have and enjoying what
we have already accomplished. Think about this for a
moment; the more that we own, the more we have to
insure it, store it, protect it, polish it, and keep it from
being stolen.

As an adjective, the word content means a state of peaceful happiness. As a verb it means to satisfy, and as a noun, a state of satisfaction. So, to be content means to be satisfied with what you have, where you are in life and at peace knowing nothing is lacking. To me, this state of acceptance of the way things are right now seems more realistic as a way of life than always chasing after something that may never become a reality. So how do we learn contentment? I suppose that we would have to start by looking at our own lives and where we are at any particular moment in time. Do you have family and friends in your life? Be content with them. Do you have money to buy food and clothing? Be content with what you have. Do you have a place to live with heat and hot water? Be content where you live. I guess the lesson here is you don't have to be a millionaire to be content, and you don't have to be famous to be content. There are many stories of rich and famous people who were miserable and far from content. The Holy Scriptures also teach that a man's life does not consist in the amount of possessions he has.[14]

There is something very normal about achieving success and being the best that we can be. It's in our very nature to strive to be better and to provide for our loved ones. It's common to want to work hard while we are young so that we have something set aside for our future when we are no longer able to work, or decide not to, so that we can enjoy our retirement years. But sometimes it's easy to lose

---

[14] Lu. 12:15 International Standard Version

our focus and forget when to stop. Each of us must decide for ourselves when to stop chasing, and when to enjoy the fruits of our labor. There are a few things we can do to practice being content. First, be grateful for one thing today and give thanks for it. Next, look in the mirror and accept who you are right now and be okay with it. Stop comparing yourself to others or unrealistic expectations of who you want to look like. You are perfect just the way you are. Accept it and move on. Last, think of those who are in your life and the people who love you. Be appreciative of them and let them know. Be content today and know that your life is good.

Do not spoil what you have by desiring what you have not; remember that what you now have was once among the things you only hoped for. —Epicurus

15

BE HONEST

Always tell the truth. That way you don't have to remember what you said. —Mark Twain

When I was just a boy my mother quoted that phrase to me, although at the time I just assumed it belonged to my mom. After all, she was the smartest person that I knew, and if she said it, it must be true. It seemed like sound advice and it actually made sense to my young mind. If I always tell the truth then I never have to remember what I said, because at least I will remember what happened, the way that it actually happened. That I could understand. Of course, what she didn't tell me was that there were consequences for also telling the truth and being brutally honest. Sometimes it didn't seem like being honest was all that it was cracked up to be. As the years have passed, I realize that there are different types of honesty that we all have to experience. The honesty that my mom was trying to teach me back then was always telling the truth. I remember once, my dad came to my defense when some of my co-workers accused me of lying to them. He stepped in and said, "Listen, my son may have a lot of faults, and he may not be perfect, but he is not a liar." Looking back, I guess I only heard the part about not being a liar and blocked out the rest of what he said. I realize now that my father was exercising brutal honesty while defending my young honor. In hindsight, that has been a teachable moment for me which I use often when I introspect into my own shortcomings. In other words, I have learned to take credit for the good, but be willing to see the bad. Otherwise, how can one improve?

There is another type of honesty, which is telling others what they need to hear, even if it might hurt them. This is where things can get dicey. My sister practices yoga on a daily basis and has for as long as I can remember. Some years back she shared a teaching with me that she learned in one of her meditations, and that is the Hindu teaching of *Satya* and *Ahimsa*, which when translated, mean *truth* and *do no harm*. We talked about the value of such knowledge and how it applies to our daily lives. Is it possible to speak the truth without doing any harm? This is the balancing act that we all have to deal with when it comes to telling those that we love and care about, things that they may not want to hear, or because it may hurt them. I would imagine that each of us have made the decision at times to hold off speaking our truth because we didn't want to cause a rift in the relationship. Honesty can be quite painful, but it has built within it such healing powers if it is accepted, especially when spoken with love and compassion. If someone is going down a wrong path that could hurt them and you speak up and tell them what they need to hear, you give them the opportunity to change, and quite possibly save them from the things that could eventually hurt them, or worse, destroy them. So, do you say nothing, or do you speak up? They may even hate you and despise you in the heat of the moment, but afterwards, if they take to heart what you said and change, they will come to respect you for your honesty and your truthfulness.

There is one more form of honesty and it's probably the hardest one that we have to deal with as progressive human beings. This one applies to us personally. How honest are we with ourselves? Can we see our own faults and our own shortcomings, or do we make excuses for them using self-justification, or blaming others? This is, as they say, where the rubber meets the road. Are we afraid to list our own faults as we see them? Have people told us things about ourselves that we've dismissed or discounted? Do we exaggerate when we share a story, or do we tell it like it is? Are we more concerned with other's opinions of us, or are we the best version of ourselves whether people like us or not?

I have learned many things over the years, and I have many talents that I have perfected, but I realized a long time ago, I do not know everything, and I'm okay with that. One of the most powerful statements that I use often is "I don't know". As a salesperson, people ask me questions often that I do not know the answer to, and I let them know that. I say to them, "I don't know, but let me do a little research and find that out for you." Most people respect that type of honesty and appreciate you telling them the truth. I have known some salespeople through the course of business who make things up and fabricate responses to questions they clearly do not have the answer to. There is no harm in not knowing everything.

Before we can ever truly be honest with others, we must first learn to be honest with ourselves. Today, be as honest with yourself as you can. If areas of your life need to be worked on, then be grateful that you still have time to become the best version of yourself that you can possibly be.

Speak with honesty, think with sincerity, and act with integrity. — Anonymous

16

BE POSITIVE

Positive thinking will let you do everything better than negative thinking will. — Zig Ziglar

Regardless of our attitude, we will still have to experience things in our lives that may be stressful, unpleasant or tragic. If we have to experience these times anyway, why not start off with a positive attitude instead of a negative one? This is a choice that we can opt to make when faced with difficulties. In all of life there is a perfect balance to all of nature and all of creation. Where there is darkness, we look for light. Where there is cold, we long for warmth. Where there is hate, we offer love. Where there is sorrow, we offer comfort and the list goes on. Day and night, up and down, left and right, east and west, wet and dry, and so on. Because there is an awful lot of negativity out in the world today, I would like to talk about being positive. It is the one emotion or demeanor that we can choose to wear in every single situation that we encounter.

Being positive not only makes you an easier person to be around, but it also has tremendous health benefits according to research.[15] Although there are continued studies that are exploring the effects of positive thinking and optimism on health, the personal benefits to us include an increased life span, lower rates of depression, lower levels of distress, better psychological and physical well-being, and better cardiovascular health, just to name a few. Although it's unclear as to why people experience many of these benefits, many point out that those with a positive outlook on life seem to cope with difficult situations better without being affected and overcome by stress.

Bring positivism into your daily life. Be positive at work. Work environments that foster a positive attitude outperform their negative counterparts. Salespeople who are optimistic outsell pessimistic salespeople. Think about it; who wants to buy something from someone who is negative and self-defeating? All of us can learn to be more positive in our relationships. Marriages and partnerships are much more likely to succeed when the couple experiences more positive interactions in their relationship, otherwise they are more likely to end in divorce. Being positive and optimistic opens doors and opportunities, and leaves room for miracles to happen, where being negative and pessimistic leaves people feeling small and beaten down and removes any chance for any hope or magic to appear.

---

[15] https://www.mayoclinic.org/healthy-lifestyle/stress-management/in-depth/positive-thinking/art-20043950

Ask yourself, are you a positive person or a negative person? Do you wake up with the best of intentions and a cheerful disposition, ready to tackle whatever may come your way? Or do you dread the mornings and going to work or about your business? Your attitude, whether you realize it or not, can be read and felt by everyone that you encounter, whether they say anything to you or not. There are many teachings that believe that all the universe and every being, creature and plant on it sends out vibrations that can be felt. When a person's disposition is either positive or negative, they actually emit vibrations that can be felt by others. If you think positive thoughts, you send out positive vibrations to those you are thinking about. The same goes for negative thoughts.

So, today are you a *glass-half-full* sort of person, or are you a *glass-half-empty* sort of person? I know it's easy to be positive when everything is going great, but the real challenge that we must face is to be positive when things aren't looking so good and not going in our favor. If we can, this shows the quality of our character and it's actually a behavior that we can get better at by practice. To put this truth into action, I chose the wise words of Norman Vincent Peale because I couldn't have said it better myself. *"The way to happiness: keep your heart free from hate, your mind from worry. Live simply, expect little, give much. Fill your life with love. Scatter sunshine. Forget self, think of others. Do as you would be done by. Try this for a week and you will be surprised."* — The Power of Positive Thinking

17

BE OUTSTANDING

Outstanding isn't something a person has, it's something a person does.[16]

There is a popular motivational quote circling cyberspace that says, "in a world full of average, be outstanding", but what does it mean to be outstanding? The dictionary defines *it as standing out from a group*, with synonyms being *noticeable, remarkable and prominent.*[17] So how does one become outstanding in their life, their career, and their relationships? I suppose one of the easiest ways to understand what it means to be outstanding is to look at some of the similar traits possessed by those we consider to be outstanding and then learn by their example.[18]

---

[16] Sherrie Campbell, 3/1/18, https://www.entrepreneur.com/article/309638
[17] https://www.merriam-webster.com/dictionary/outstanding
[18] '8 Traits of Outstanding People', https://www.entrepreneur.com/article/309638

First, we have the three "P's". Purpose, passion and perseverance. Outstanding people have a very clear sense of purpose in both their public and private lives. They develop a clear vision of what they want and then they hold on tight to that vision and remain unnerved, unswayed and focused on that purpose. Next, they have a genuine passion for what they want to accomplish, whether it be personal, financial or global. This is their dream and they willingly sacrifice anything to achieve that dream. They don't let naysayers get in their way and they are passionate about life--period. Outstanding people don't just survive this life, they thrive while enjoying this life. Another quality of outstanding people is that they don't quit when the going gets tough. They don't make excuses for things getting difficult. These people persevere. They know the cost of what they are reaching for, they dig their heels in and they brace themselves for setbacks and for failure along the way. They are realists and they prepare in advance for disappointments, because they realize to attain what they are striving for will take blood, sweat and tears, but they also know that there is a light at the end of the tunnel.

Another trait of outstanding people is that they wake up every morning with a choice just like you and me. The difference between them and the rest of the world is that outstanding people choose to be positive and embrace life every single day. Outstanding people choose not to be rattled by setbacks, knowing the only way to truly learn from past mistakes is to not repeat them. They choose to see their weaknesses and embrace their fears.

Once they know their weaknesses they adapt and get better at their craft. Look at it, accept it and move on. Outstanding people use every opportunity to hone their skills, especially failure. For they know that only by accepting failure as part of the journey, can they get stronger in the face of adversity, for nothing worthwhile is ever easy. Another telltale characteristic of outstanding people is their optimism. They are the poster child for living positive thinking. How can anyone expect to realize their dreams or achieve their goals if they do not possess hope and confidence? Outstanding people see the glass half full and they see their journey, with all of its twists and turns, as worth it for the prize at the end of the run. Optimism is the ability to see the successful outcome of the future with hope and confidence. This is some of what it takes to be outstanding.

I am the type of person that gives one hundred percent and more towards any job or task that I am about to undertake. I make it an effort to give my best performance, my best effort, and by best skills whatever I am involved in working on. There is a bible scripture that says whatever your hand finds to do, do it with all your might, [19] meaning give your best all the time without settling for just okay. We may not consider ourselves to outstanding, and that's probably fine. I want to know, that no matter what, I chose to give it my all and would not settle for anything less than my very best.

---

[19] Ecc.9:10, New International Version

Being outstanding isn't about wealth, it isn't about status, and it isn't about fame. It's about being the best that you can be with whatever you set out to do. It's about not letting failure ruin you or naysayers sway you. It's about defining a purpose, holding on to that purpose with passion, with hope and with confidence and sticking to the course, no matter how hard it gets. It's about never quitting and believing in the impossible and believing in yourself. It's about seeing the future before it happens and actually making it happen through your own hard work, your own sweat, and your own vision.

Today is an opportunity to define your dreams, set your goals and gear up for the journey to maximize your potential. So many people wait until it's too late in life or think that they are too old to realize the many things they wanted to achieve and probably could have, had they gone after what they wanted in life. I don't know about you, but I never wanted to be most people. I wanted to be outstanding!

Outstanding people have one thing in common: an absolute sense of mission. — Zig Ziglar

18

BE TRUSTWORTHY

Be loyal and trustworthy. Do not befriend anyone who is lower than yourself in this regard. — Confucius

It's been said that trust is a very fragile thing. Easy to lose, easy to break, and very difficult to ever get back. I would imagine that all of us have had experiences where either we broke someone's trust, or someone broke ours, and the friendship or relationship suffered the consequences. When a trust is broken it has a way of setting a new benchmark for those who were hurt, and it makes someone less trusting the next time around. There are different types of trusts that we all have had to experience, and they each have their part in our life. The first type of trust is between spouses, partners or lovers. I call this the "marriage trust." It's an unspoken bond that the love and relationship that you share is exclusive and not to be treated lightly or trampled on. It is to be revered, respected, and at all costs, protected. When this type of trust is broken, it very often leads to separation and divorce, because how can you trust someone a second time around if that person has already hurt you or cheated on you? Very few relationships can survive a cheating partner, and it's nothing short of a miracle when one does. I would guess it's better not to take that chance and remain loyal to one person for as long as you are in that relationship. If you are unhappy with the person with whom you share this bond, then be honest and end the relationship. It's far better to hurt someone by being honest with them, than to lie to someone and cheat on them. At least you will be on moral high ground, whatever the outcome of the relationship.

Another type of trust is that between family, friends and coworkers that I call the "friendship trust." This is about keeping and holding another's secrets or personal feelings and not blabbing them or sharing them with others. This is also called, keeping someone's confidence. When someone puts their trust in you and opens up about personal things, they are really saying "I trust you enough to share with you the things that I do not want to share with others." I have found over the course of my life, when I am able to share my personal feelings with someone, they are more apt to want to share their private or personal feelings with me. Trust is a two-way street. If one person does all the sharing and the other is unwilling to open up, eventually people catch on and stop opening up. It's probably because of vulnerability. If you know all my secrets and I know nothing about yours, you have a lot of control over the relationship and what you can do with the knowledge that you possess. The friendship trust is also difficult to regain and repair once it has been violated. I have seen and experienced relationships that had lasted twenty, thirty, and forty years end in a moment because of broken trust. The best way to trust someone is to take a chance and trust them.

The last type of trust is something that I call the "career trust or business trust." This includes how you handle your work, how you handle customers and those you work with, and how you handle money that does not belong to you. Are you honest with your time and the hours that you work, or do you fudge it a little every now and then? Are you honest with customers and your co-workers, or do you lie just a little or exaggerate just to appease a situation? How honest are you with other people's money? Each of us must ask ourselves these questions, and only we have the power to be the best that we can be in every situation and opportunity that presents itself to us. I have seen people take advantage of situations at their job and get fired, and depending on the severity of their actions, some have even had difficulty getting employed again because some offenses can follow a person for years and affect their future employment.

Trustworthy people are sincere, they are authentic, and they have tremendous integrity. These are the people that say what they mean and mean what they say. They can be counted on to always tell you just the way that it is without candy-coating anything. They are always true to themselves and they don't ever try to be something that they are not, nor do they try and be someone else. These are the people that always choose to do the right thing, even when no one is looking. Trustworthy people have a consistency about them, and people know that they can count on them. They are not chameleons who are constantly changing color to please someone, instead they are firm, genuine, and steadfast in their beliefs. I would imagine that most people like to be around this type of person, so it's a quality that we all can, and should aspire to possess. How trustworthy of a person are you, and how trustworthy of a person do you want to be? We all have the power to change and get better with each passing day.

Today, try to be more trusting with people, not only those that you know, but also with those that you do not know. Assume the best about someone without letting prejudice or preconceptions come into play.

To be trusted is a greater compliment than being loved. — George MacDonald

19

BE NON-JUDGMENTAL

Be curious, not judgmental. — Walt Whitman

For the past few days before writing this essay, I have been thinking about this topic and what it takes to become a non-judgmental person, all the time, in every situation that I encounter. In light of this, I was pondering the opposite of judgement. If we were discussing sentencing or punishment, I suppose mercy would be the opposite. But I am more interested in how it relates to the theme of this writing, and as I was meditating on the inspirational words that I have read, it seems to me that *observation* would be the closest opposite of judgment in light of these short essays. While observation is the act of observing something in order to gain information, judgement is an opinion or conclusion that we form based on what we observed. Many times, throughout our life we think we are observing someone or something, but in reality, we are already forming opinions of what we are seeing, quite possibly without us ever being aware that we are doing this. We end up appointing ourselves judge and jury and making conclusions with our mind, while all the while shutting our hearts to the person or the situation. Elvis Presley once said, *"to judge a person by their weakest attribute, is like judging the power of the ocean by one wave."* It's the same with us as people. If we are to be judged by our weakest moment or our greatest fault, that doesn't show an accurate picture of who we are over the course of a lifetime. On the timeline of our lives, it's merely a fragment, or a blip on the screen, and it doesn't even begin to describe the person that we truly are.

Looking back at my own experiences, I realize now that although I was unaware at the time, I would judge people by what I assumed they should be doing, or how they should be acting. It wasn't until I found myself on the receiving end of being found fault with and judged by people in my own life, who had no idea what I was going through, that made me aware of how I had done the very same thing many years prior. I realize that I cannot go back and undo my past, but I can learn from my experiences and become a better individual by not assuming that I know what's best for someone, unless my counsel or my advice has been solicited. So how do we learn to be less judgmental and more accepting and open to others? One way that I have found is through meditation or introspection.

Although there are different types of meditation, the one I am speaking of here is sitting quietly for five to ten minutes alone somewhere away from any chaos or noise and just breathe. This exercise is meant to help me focus on only my breathing and block out everything else. What takes place in the brain while this is happening is a shift from beta brain waves to theta brain waves.[20] Beta brain waves are typically present in people in non-meditative states, where it's easier to become anxious, depressed or stressed out. In this state, we typically form quick opinions of others without fully understanding the situation, causing us to be more judgmental of others. However, when you meditate or quietly introspect, you activate the theta brain waves which allows you to become more accepting and open to others, and less judgmental toward them. Theta brain waves help us become more connected to the universe, more inspired and more at peace with life, and when we are more content and peaceful, we see things differently, like looking through rose-colored glasses. Things appear better.

Because each human being is so diverse and so unique from another, there is no possible way for us to know what others are experiencing and dealing with by just noticing them or passing by them, therefore it's impossible to form an opinion of someone by the way that they are dressed, or how tall or short they are, or how thin or overweight they are, or what nationality or religion they are. No two people are exactly alike in their thoughts, their feelings or their emotions, so it's ludicrous to think that we can form an opinion about someone without first sitting down with them, listening to them, and getting to know them through their life's experiences. Once we do, and if we

---

[20] https://lucid.me/blog/5-brainwaves-delta-theta-alpha-beta-gamma/

are exercising compassion, there's no room for judgment or fault finding any longer. Take yourself for example: how many strangers know what you are going through today, or the difficulties that you are facing? How could a stranger ever know the heartache and sadness you are carrying? What if you just landed your dream job today and you are giddy and excited beyond words, and simply high on life? What would someone who doesn't know you say or think about you today, if that's all they saw? For someone to pass judgment on you without knowing you because of how you look or how you act is just plain senseless, and if you knew, would probably bother you. This is how we make others feel when we do the same thing. Even Jesus taught his disciples not to judge. He went on to say, "if you judge someone, you will be judged in the same manner as how you passed judgment." [21]

Choose a day to be an observer instead of a judge and be aware of how many times you form an opinion of someone or something simply on the outward appearance. At that very moment, catch yourself while it's happening and stop. Take a moment and learn from it. Immediately send kind thoughts and compassion to whomever you were just passing an opinion on and choose observation instead of judgment. Also, take a few minutes throughout your day to be quiet and rest and meditate on just breathing. Remember, in this state we are more prone to kind thoughts, lighter emotions, and increased positivism toward all living things. Just as we wouldn't want people

---

[21] Mt.7:1,2 Berean Study Bible

forming opinions of us without knowing us, we in turn shouldn't pass judgement on others based on outward appearance. Be a person who sends kindness and love to all creatures and to all creation. Like my parents always taught me, it's best not to judge anyone, because we really don't know what someone else is going through. Take the time to love people. Just because someone is a complete stranger to you, doesn't mean that they couldn't use a little kindness and a little warmth. Plato, one of the greatest philosophers once was quoted saying "be kind, for everyone you meet is fighting a hard battle."

What is love? Love is the absence of judgment. — Dalai Lama

20

HELP A STRANGER

There are no strangers here; Only friends you haven't yet met.
— William Butler Yeats

Think about all of the friends that you have accumulated over the many years of your life, and yet how often do we forget that at one time, many of those close friends started out as complete strangers to us. If not for some form of communication and spending time together, a friendship may not have ever been forged. Of course I am not suggesting that every stranger needs to become your friend, but many of us get so involved in our own lives and the day to day routines, I can't help but wonder if we miss opportunities every day to help a complete stranger that happens to wander across our path while on this journey. There is much to be said on this topic and many a person have spoken words of wisdom to encourage us to be a help in times of need. When we help others without any expectation of anything in return, we actually feed our own souls with the benefits of life, health and positive energy.

A few months ago I was exiting the interstate and I noticed a young man near the exit of the ramp holding a sign that read "Homeless and hungry". I immediately felt saddened that in a country as prosperous and blessed as these United States of America, there are so many people without food, without shelter, and given the time of year that I saw him, without the necessary warmth that many of us may take for granted. Without hesitation I reached into my wallet, pulled out what I had, and handed it to him while I was waiting for the traffic light to turn to green. As I drove away, I said a silent prayer for him, and I took a few moments to thank God for everything that I had. It was a humbling experience for me knowing that 'there but by the grace of God, go I.' That's why, each morning that I wake, before my feet hit the floor, I say the words "Thank you for life and health today." This sets a benchmark of appreciation for the rest of the day.

There are many ways that we can help people that we don't know. Our town has a local community services center that gathers clothing, furniture, donations and food and redistributes them to needy families right here in our hometown. They depend on the generosity of people to keep their work alive. Each year around the holidays my wife and I donate grocery gift cards as well as anything else that we hear that they need to brighten a family's spirits. Even Paul the apostle wrote in his epistle to the Hebrews, "be not forgetful to entertain strangers: for thereby some have entertained angels unawares." We may never get to know the people that we help, but our acts of kindness will never be forgotten.

I remember when I was a kid, we would take long road trips in the car together, and when we came to a toll plaza, many times my dad would pay for our car and the car behind us. As we pulled away from the toll plaza the car that he paid for would catch up to us and honk the horn and wave as if to say thank you. This event happened more times than not and each time us kids would watch with excitement when the people realized that my dad had just paid their toll for them. It's one of the fondest memories that I have of my dad and when I began to drive, and when our state still had toll plazas, I did the very same thing a few times just because my dad did. I wanted to see what it felt like. Today they call it random acts of kindness and it still feels great. I learned a lot about helping strangers from my parents. I saw my mother pay for a woman's groceries one day when she saw that the woman in front of her didn't have enough money to cover it. The woman broke into tears and sobbed while thanking my mom. It's a memory that I'll never forget. Another time, I watched my dad pay for dinner for a family at a restaurant because he could tell the man didn't have enough to pay the check. The man was so touched and so humbled that he too began to cry and shake my dad's hand and thank him. These moments have stayed with me for years and I often try and emulate the kindness and the unselfishness that my parents exhibited on more than one occasion. For me, these are 'pay it forward' moments that can truly clear the cobwebs out of any dusty old wallet and teach generosity.

If you're ever feeling the blues and find yourself in a slump, and you need a real 'pick-me-up', do something unexpected and kind for a complete stranger. I promise you; your blues will fade, and your slump will disappear. I've read that when a butterfly flaps its wings, that energy flows thousands of miles away. Therefore, everything you think and do extends outward and multiplies.[22] We are beings with tremendous power and tremendous energy, because we are what we came from. Charles Dickens once said, "No one is useless in this world who lightens the burdens of another." Today, why not help a stranger? Be useful and help someone who needs your kindness and your compassion. Trust me--the reward far outweighs the cost.

If a man be gracious and courteous to strangers, it shows he is a citizen of the world, and that his heart is no island cut off from other lands, but a continent that joins them. — Sir Francis Bacon

---

[22] Change Your Thoughts - Change Your Life, Verse 54, pg. 264, Dr. Wayne Dyer

21

BE FAITHFUL

A faithful friend is a strong defense; And he that hath found him hath found a treasure. — Louisa May Alcott

When you think of someone being faithful, what comes to your mind? What does be faithful really mean to you? What qualities does someone possess that makes them a faithful person? How does one become faithful? Are there different ways of being faithful? For starters, the word faithful means being loyal, being true, being firm in devotion to something or someone united by some type of a promise, commitment or pledge. People can be faithful to a cause like saving the whales and keeping our oceans free of pollution. Others take up protecting the environment by only driving eco-friendly cars, or recycling, or only purchasing sustainable products. A person can be faithful to their spouse or partner by not cheating on them, not flirting while out in public, and honoring the vows that were made between them. The relationships that are the most difficult to repair are the ones where one partner was unfaithful to the other and like I mentioned earlier, these are almost impossible to recover from. In my lifetime I've seen more than my fair share of these types of relationships end in divorce, separation, and eventually disaster. What's sad is that it was avoidable by just honoring the commitments that were made. Nothing more and nothing less, just being faithful to the vows that were made.

One can also be faithful to a belief in God, Allah, the Universe, or some other higher power, and subsequently they choose to live a life that aligns with the belief system of that higher power such as keeping the commandments of God, obeying the teachings of Allah, or living a life of kindness towards all creatures and all creation, honoring mother Earth. Action must follow commitment otherwise the promises are empty, and the words are meaningless. Be willing to stand for something that you believe in and be willing to fight for a cause, especially when it's not convenient. This is the real test of the faithful. Remaining loyal and true to the end, regardless of the outcome. Every martyr died faithful unto death for the cause that they believed in. Their lives depicted faithfulness in action. Alexander Hamilton is quoted saying, "If you don't stand for something, you will fall for anything." I would say that these are powerful words that put this truth into proper perspective.

Then there are those people who are faithful friends. These special individuals are loyal to the end, these are the people who will stand with you when others run for the hills, and these are the people who will defend your honor in your absence, and those who you can trust with your life. Jesus said, "Greater love has no one than this, that someone lay down his life for his friends."[23] I've read that such people can be a rare find, but they're out there, probably more of them than you think, you just haven't met them yet. In the book of Proverbs, it is written, "Many a man proclaims his own steadfast love, but a faithful man who can find?"[24] So it begs the question, are you a faithful friend? Are you a faithful employee? Are you someone who can be trusted to remain loyal and honor your promises when the going gets tough? I've asked myself those same questions many times throughout my life and let's just say that the answer is progressive like a moving target that changes, for the better, over time. I suppose the truth is, the older I get, the more wisdom I acquire, and life's lessons teach me how to be a better person. Am I a faithful friend? I would say that I am more faithful now than I was twenty years ago and getting better at it every day. I have always tried to be a man of my word and keep my promises, but one lesson that I have learned over the years is to only make promises that I intend to keep, and that I know I can keep. I've learned that honesty is more important to me than making empty promises. Am I faithful in my job and my business? I would again say that I am more faithful now than I was twenty years ago. I present my customers with what they asked for, I tell them the truth, and I've made it a habit to never sell someone anything that they don't need. I never

---

[23] John 15:13, English Standard Version
[24] Prov. 20:6, English Standard Version

misrepresent, and I don't "candy-coat" the truth just to make a sale. I give people the same courtesy that I would want by telling them the truth, even if it's not what they want to hear. Most people that I have encountered would rather hear the truth anyway, and find a way to deal with it, than being told lies. People respect me for telling them the truth.

I have learned that being faithful becomes a way of life, and it starts with being honest with yourself. Look inside your heart, search your soul, see who you are, realize what you want to become, and then live that life accordingly. Be faithful and loyal to the beliefs that you profess. If you are interested in a particular cause, be faithful to that cause, and help out when needed to bring more attention to that cause. If you are in a relationship, be faithful to your partner. Honor the vows that you made and be a person of absolute integrity. Always choose the right way, even when no one is looking. If you want to be more trusted at your job and given more responsibility, be faithful in the small things that you are assigned, and over time, your faithfulness will be rewarded. When we begin to be faithful to ourselves first, keeping the promises that we make to ourselves, then we can be faithful to others. The Brazilian novelist Paulo Coelho said it best— "If you want to be faithful to someone, start by being faithful to yourself."

Hold faithfulness and sincerity as first principles. — Confucius

22

BE HOPEFUL

The natural flights of the human mind are not from pleasure to pleasure, but from hope to hope. — Samuel Johnson

Being hopeful means that you are feeling or inspiring optimism about a future event.[25] I would imagine that most of us have gone through some difficult times and most likely experienced one or two dark nights of the soul. I'm also guessing that chances are pretty good that some glimmer of hope, or some light at the end of that dark tunnel kept us going and gave us the strength that we needed to carry on, when in fact we may have felt like giving up. Being hopeful means that you don't give up and you don't quit. Being hopeful means that the glass is usually more than half full. It also means that the chances of succeeding at something far outweigh the chances of failing. Similar to optimism, being hopeful is the tendency to always expect a favorable outcome.

---

[25] www.lexico.com/definition/hopeful

When I was in my teens and much less experienced with life as I am today, I was always quite optimistic and hopeful. I believed that good always triumphs over evil. I believed that it was always darkest just before dawn. I believed that people who do the right thing and follow the rules always win in the end and come out ahead. As I have matured and experienced my share of heartache and sadness, I've questioned my hopefulness at times throughout my life. Through some of the experiences that I have been through, I have seen the dark side of human nature, where, at times, good and decent people are punished and hurt, while bad people seem to prosper and thrive. I suppose that this goes back to the age-old question, "Why do bad things happen to good people?" While I do not have the answer to this question to satisfy everyone who would ask, I have tried to find my own answer deep within my heart and make peace with my understanding of it. The conclusion that I have come to that helps me get through difficult times, is that my life is a journey, and along this journey there are going to be difficulties and heartaches. Not once did my parents or teachers ever tell me that life will be perfect and you will make it through unscathed, or that the way to happiness is all downhill. I have come to accept that there is a balance in life. While we may experience sorrow and hurt, we also have times of incredible joy and pleasure. This is life and it's our choice on how to live it. My mother once said, "life is meant to be lived, so go out and live your life." We can choose to wallow in the hurt forever, or we can develop an attitude of hopefulness and optimistic expectation, knowing that there is going to be hurt and heartache, but with a hopeful outlook, we will find the strength and the know-how to accept those times and get through them. That's called being real and seeing things for what they are.

It's funny to me how the things that we hope for change or adapt to our individual lives as we move forward on this journey. When I was younger the things that I was hopeful about were more of a materialistic nature and mean little or nothing to me now. I realize that it's not so much *what* I am hopeful about, but rather, being optimistic and hopeful in general. Having a positive outlook on life seems to make the trek a little more enjoyable and a little less stressful. Of the many self-help books that I have read over the years on being successful, there is a common teaching, that if we spend time with people who are positive, successful and motivated, we tend to become more positive, more successful and more motivated ourselves. If we believe that we can, chances are, we can. The same is true in reverse. When people are fighting unhealthy addictions and bad behaviors, the first thing that's recommended for them to implement on their road to recovery is to stay away from the people, the places and the things that influenced their poor choices and fueled their addiction in the first place. Having a support system in place with hopeful, positive people can do wonders for those looking to improve their lives.

If you are struggling with being hopeful and being optimistic about the future, there are a few things that you can do to help. First, change your outlook. Instead of assuming bad things are going to happen, find joy and happiness in little things that make you smile. It could be a glass of wine, or your favorite song, or a warm fire on cold winter's night. Either way, when we change the way we look at something, our thoughts change. If we can catch ourselves when we are talking negatively, we can stop at that very moment and speak more optimistically. Our brains are extremely impressionable and quite adaptive to our thoughts and our speech. If that little voice in our head is negative, our brains can actually turn genes on or off in our bodies and stimulate a litany of other chemical reactions, including the release of cortisol, the stress hormone, causing us even more discomfort. The opposite effect is also true. Holistic Health Practitioner and author, Dr. Julie Scalise, says, "Just thinking or talking to yourself, either positively or negatively, has an effect on all physical structures in our body, not just our mood or emotions." She goes on to say, "when we talk positive and think positive our brains release more Serotonin which is responsible for keeping anxiety in check, greater feelings of self-worth, as well as Dopamine which promotes motivation, interest, and drive." [26] When we think positive and are hopeful about coming events, we actually improve our overall health and well-being. The good news is that we can start today being more hopeful and being more optimistic. The health benefits alone are worth it. Remember, as long as there is breath, there is hope. Today is great because you are alive and you are here, and tomorrow can only get better!

Hope is the dream of a waking man. — Aristotle

---

[26] www.brainspeak.com/how-megative-self-talk-sabotages-your-health-happiness

23

FIND LOVE

Never love anyone who treats you like you're ordinary. — Oscar Wilde

On the topic of love, there are more songs written and sung about it than any other topic. There are thousands of quotes on the topic of love, hundreds and hundreds of movies and television shows about love, not to mention more greeting cards on the subject of love than just about any other. In fact, online research shows that in 2019, American consumers spent over $20 billion on Valentine's Day alone, and that's up six percent from the previous year. So, what is it about this wonderful, intense emotion that can bring us so much tremendous joy in one moment, and yet cause us so much heartache at another?

One of the most rewarding, yet most difficult things to do is to love someone unconditionally, to give them your heart, and let them know it. This can also create feelings of vulnerability, which may be part of the reason that many people find it difficult to make that type of commitment, especially if they've been hurt by love in the past. As the saying goes, once bitten, twice shy. In my own experience, maybe part of the problem in finding and holding on to love, is because we set our own expectations of what we want and then imagine who will embody the qualities that we are looking for. Many times, our expectations may be unrealistic, and when things don't materialize the way we thought they should, we get disappointed and discouraged with love. One of the most beautiful things to watch is young, innocent love blossom because the two involved have no real experience with being hurt by love, so they enter into this relationship with a 'devil-may-care' blind simplicity and they simply enjoy the ride. There's a lesson to be learned here and if we want to find love and be loved, we must be willing to throw a little caution to the wind and take a chance.

So how can we learn to embody the true essence of love and become beings that really know how to love? Of all the writings and research available on how to become better at loving, nothing teaches the basics better than the famous Bible passage in First Corinthians about love. It provides a simple outline for us that teaches that love is patient, love is kind, and love does not envy.[27] Are you patient and kind to your spouse or partner? Are you jealous or envious of something that your partner has, or can do better than you? If you can find weaknesses in your love, work to change them. Become better at love by putting these first truths into practice in your own relationships. When you

---

[27] 1 Cor. 13:1-13 King James Version

do, you begin to embody some of the characteristics of genuine love by living them. It goes onto say that love does not boast or brag, and it's not proud. Love does not dishonor others, nor is it self-seeking. It's always best to remain humble and put your partner's needs above your own needs. If both parties are applying this truth, there is little room for tension, because each is seeking the happiness of the other. Each of these qualities, when added into our relationships, helps to bring out the best in others, and keeps us humble, and willing to serve. Love is not easily angered, nor does it keep any records of any past wrong doings. Keeping our cool in the heat of an argument or disagreement can work wonders for the successful outcome of any situation. Never, under any circumstances should you bring up someone's past mistakes and throw them in their face. This is probably the worst thing that you can do, on par with pouring gasoline into a raging fire, and it will certainly bring about a disaster that won't easily be diffused. Love always protects, it always trusts, it always hopes, and it always perseveres. Love does not quit. Love never fails, it always endures.

Love is more than just a fleeting emotion of longing or lustful passion. Love is more than just casual sex or a random intimate desire. I've been married for over twenty years, and the love that my wife and I share has grown over time and has taught us both what loving someone really means. It's more than the youthful emotions that get swept away with a kiss or a touch. It's more than public displays of affection, and it's much more than what we are conditioned to believe from watching movies. My wife and I have been through hundreds and hundreds of experiences, and real-life situations, many of them extremely difficult to bear, both individually and on our marriage. Many of them constantly put our love to the test and made us take a step back and question ourselves as to whether or not we were keeping to our promises or looking for a way out. The one thing that kept us grounded was our ability to talk things out and we enjoy spending time together. A short time after we were married, we would wake every morning and have coffee together spending the first hour or so before heading to work sharing, talking or just being together. What started as just morning coffee, has actually become a way of life for us, and with the exception of one of us traveling or being out of town, we have never missed a morning in over twenty years having coffee together. Perhaps it's our silent way of saying "I'm here and I'm not going anywhere." Being with someone who has become my best friend, and my closest confidant is what I associate with lasting love.

If you happen to be one of those individuals who are still searching for your soulmate, chances are you are already experiencing love in many forms including the love of family, best friends, and believe it or not, animals. Many of the same dynamics apply when it comes to these relationships. As humans, our nature is quite adaptive to our circumstances and our environment. As our life moves in and out of different phases, so also, do our relationships. The most important thing to remember is that we need to keep our heart open to love in however it appears and be ready to take a chance if the right person comes into our life.

Real and lasting love is the totality of all of these qualities becoming one in an individual, and learning to love can take years to perfect, and the road will not always be a cakewalk. Although it may almost seem too simple to put into practice, these time-honored truths have been the cornerstone of millions of successful relationships. Carlos Wallace is quoted saying, "Loving someone is a full-time commitment. Use that time wisely. Cherish the high points and fight hard to conquer the challenges. No one said love would be easy, but it is damn sure worth it."

Being deeply loved by someone gives you strength, while loving someone deeply gives you courage. — Lao Tzu

24

BE YOURSELF

Your time is limited, so don't waste it living someone else's life. — Steve Jobs

Back a few months ago, a friend of mine was commenting about a post on social media that he saw about one of his friends. He went on to share with me that as he was viewing this person's profile, he said to me, "social media only shows the highlights in a person's life." And of course, I understand that. How many people would really post on their pages about an uncle who got arrested for DUI, or a sister going through a nasty custody battle because she was caught cheating with her husband's best friend? Social media is all about the highlight reels of a person's life, which brings me to this next short essay. How can we learn to just be ourselves in all of the relationships that we have, without watering down who we are or hiding our true selves? Oscar Wilde was quoted saying, "Be yourself; everyone else is already taken." It's true, each of us are unique, and there is no one on this planet past, present or future that will ever be a carbon-copy of who we are, so why try and be someone else?

Learning to be yourself takes work, and over the course of my life I've always tried to be myself by including all of my goodness, all of my badness, and all of my uniqueness. But it's much more than just learning to be yourself, it's acceptance when you realize who you really are. Looking back at my life I suppose there were moments that I thought I wasn't good enough, or talented enough to be counted with others who were obviously more athletic, better looking, and smarter than I was. Instead of accepting I was comparing, and many times to unrealistically high standards. I would hear a lot of negative self-talk going on inside my head, and much of it I believed, or at least accepted at first. It can become quite overwhelming and destructive when negative self-talk turns into self-loathing. The quickest way to stop that toxic thinking is to find the positive and focus on our strengths, and our accomplishments. Recognize where you shine and be willing to accept the praise and the compliments that are associated with your talents and your abilities. So many times, we accept the rebuke when told about our shortcomings and our weaknesses, but we're not as accepting when people want to praise us or speak highly of us. This is called false-humility and it needs to stop. Like I mentioned earlier, we are the sum total of all of our experiences, both good and bad. Nothing can change who we have become, but only we can change who we want to become.

Part of becoming genuine, and just being who we are is learning to express ourselves, and that means being real, and unfiltered. We are who we are, and if some people don't like us, that's okay. Not everyone is going to like us, that's just a hard fact that we all need to accept. If people choose not to be around us because we are not afraid to speak our mind, we stand for our convictions, and choose not to let our past mistakes define us, then that's their prerogative, and as time will tell, it's also their loss. Being yourself includes admitting when you make a mistake and accepting responsibility when you are wrong. Everyone makes mistakes, so you are not alone. However, learning to admit when you are wrong takes guts and takes courage. Remember, weak individuals are afraid to fess up and will never admit when they are wrong, but strong, valiant people learn to fall on their own sword as many times as it takes to become a better person. You don't have to hide behind someone else's standards or opinions of who you are. There is only one you, and the world needs you just the way you are with all of your quirkiness, all of your uniqueness and all of your amazingness. Even Jesus said, "Let your light shine before men so they can see your good works, and glorify your Father, which is in Heaven."[28] Your light is your essence and your truth. It's all about who you are and your very nature, good and bad, all rolled up into one ball of flesh and blood. When you become yourself and just be who you are, the very best of you shines forth. For some it may be a light of hope that they've been searching for to guide their way because

---

[28] Matthew 5:15, New King James Version

of your truthfulness, your honesty and your real-life's experiences. For others it may be an intense searchlight, or a probe into their darkness and their hidden secrets, for which you may be the irritation that they need to avoid. Whatever the case may be, never stop being who you are, never stop letting your light shine, regardless of the outcome. At the end of each day, the only person that you need to answer to is yourself. We all know when we've made a difference in another's life, and we all know when we have fallen short of being the best person we could be in any given moment. We don't need anyone else tearing us apart or reminding us how badly we've behaved. Chances are, we already know it. If we are honest with ourselves and take to heart our own criticism, we can improve and do better next time. Each night before I go to sleep, I say a prayer and take an account of my days actions and see how it all played out. If I realize that I spoke to someone in harsh words, I ask for forgiveness and send a silent prayer of kindness to that person. Atonement is another defining quality of people of character and you are a person of character when you are being real, when you are standing strong in your convictions, and when you are just simply--being yourself.

"If you celebrate your differentness, the world will, too. It believes exactly what you tell it—through the words you use to describe yourself, the actions you take to care for yourself, and the choices you make to express yourself. Tell the world you are one-of-a-kind creation who came here to experience wonder and spread joy. Expect to be accommodated." — Victoria Moran, Lit from Within: Tending Your Soul for Lifelong Beauty

To be yourself in a world that is constantly trying to make you something else is the greatest accomplishment. — Ralph Waldo Emerson

Epilogue

When you are content to be simply yourself and don't compare or compete, everyone will respect you. — Lao Tzu

The idea for this book came to me a few months ago as I was meditating quietly about my life and the road that I have traveled this far. I was making a mental list of many of the things that I have learned through my life's experiences, and those that I have adopted into my life as qualities of a person that I had always hoped to one day personify. I sat down one beautiful autumn morning and began to make a list of those qualities that helped me improve my life and then decided to put my thoughts onto paper and share with you my experiences on how I have tried to integrate these positive traits into my own life on a daily basis. My goal wasn't to write a novel that took a year to read, filled with plot twists and cliff hangers, but rather a simple guidebook where you could read one essay a day and then in quiet meditation or prayer, if you chose to do so, implement the truths contained in that short essay without being overwhelmed to be, or do anything, other than just be yourself.

Although my original list was much longer, I decided to settle on these twenty-four qualities and the short essays that follow, mostly because these stood out to me as characteristics that I see as part of a God-realized life. I also saw these as a means of providing a sort of daily mantra or topic of meditation for those that like that sort of thing, I know, I do. I wanted to make them short and easy to read so they could be added into one's daily routine. The content of each essay is, for the most part, simple and straightforward.

While I was writing these essays, I would share them each day with my sister, the educator, who became my audience of one, and my best critic. As someone who practices yoga each day, she is familiar with the concept of introducing a daily mantra or meditation into one's routine. Her input has been invaluable to me, and I am grateful for her participation in this project. She has encouraged me to keep on track and to get this book completed in a timely manner. She has offered her literary expertise every now and again, to which I most graciously accepted.

At the end of the essays, there is an opportunity to implement these truths and ideas on how to put them into practice. These are, of course, my own humble opinions, and you are welcome to integrate them any way that you like that works for you. Like I mentioned in the introduction, these short essays are meant to be type of a "refresher course" in the basics of human nature. I've always been of the belief that there is always room for improvement and if someone has an idea that can help me become a better person, then so be it. I leave you with this quote from my dad. "Never stop learning, you're not done yet."

Thank you for reading this book and thank you for allowing me to share some of my experiences with you. I wish you peace and health in your journey here. May you always have a connection to the Divine source from which we all originated.

Namaste!

About the Author

With almost six decades of experience, Dan has learned a lot about life as a limo driver, car salesman, composer, songwriter, recording engineer, inspirational teacher, artist, painter, carpenter, magazine publisher, designer, husband, brother and a friend. Through his experiences, both positive and negative, he has learned to adapt and become flexible with every situation he has found himself in and always tries to find the best in each of those moments. His writings are honest and light-hearted, yet powerfully poignant. You almost feel as if he's in the room with you, laughing, sharing stories and personal experiences, and accepting that life is short, and that we need to treasure each moment. In this little book of daily verses, he encourages his reader to take to heart each one and to make them a part of your daily routines.

Dan's writing style has you feel as if he is sitting down with you sharing a conversation with old friends. It's apparent that through his heartaches and his life struggles, he has softened with a compassionate grace towards all living things--and it's evident in each of his personal life stories how he's found inner peace with where he is in his life's journey. He sees himself as his brother's keeper and takes seriously the welfare of those with whom he comes into contact. His hope is that these short writings can help people live a more God-realized life, bringing them the peace, joy, and happiness that each of us deserves. If just one person achieves that, then his life has been successful.

Printed in the United States
By Bookmasters